"Whispers of a Gentle Soul"

Jaya Shree Devkar

BookLeaf Publishing

India | USA | UK

Presentation by *BookLeaf Publishing*

Web: www.bookleafpub.com

E-mail: info@bookleafpub.com

ISBN:9789360942137

First edition 2024

DEDICATION

ACKNOWLEDGEMENT

In crafting "Whispers of a Gentle Soul," I stand indebted to the multitude of influences that have shaped this collection. To those who have touched my life, my gratitude knows no bounds. Firstly, immense appreciation for the silent muses who reside within us all—the resilient souls who inspire these verses. Your stories, courage, and unwavering spirit illuminate these pages.

A heartfelt thank you to my family, whose unwavering support provided the foundation for my creative endeavors. Your love and encouragement have been my guiding stars. To my friends, the pillars of laughter and solace, thank you for being the backdrop to my life's composition. Your camaraderie has added vibrant hues to the canvas of my journey. A special note of gratitude to the literary community—authors, poets, and mentors—who have paved the way for my growth. Your words have been a source of both inspiration and enlightenment. To the readers, your willingness to embark on this poetic voyage warms my heart. May these verses resonate with the chords of your own experiences.

Lastly, to the team who contributed to the realization of this book—editors, designers, and publishers—your dedication and expertise have transformed words into a tangible creation.

PREFACE

In the delicate cadence of these verses, we embark on a journey that transcends time—a journey into the heart and soul of a woman whose life unfolds in the lines of poetry. The preface serves as an invitation to step into the world of "Whispers of a Gentle Soul," offering a glimpse into the inspiration, the dreams, and the unyielding spirit that birthed each poetic chapter. As you turn the pages, may you find solace, inspiration, and a mirror reflecting the resilience inherent in every human spirit.

Table of Contents

Songs of Innocence in a Shadowed World

In whispers soft, a tale unfolds,
Of innocence, in a world so cold.
She yearns for skies forever blue,
A childhood dream, so pure and true.

Radiant Kindness

In a world of chaos, she shines bright,
Her kindness a beacon, her heart pure light.
With a smile, she melts every strife,
In her grace, we find solace, love thrives.

Echoes of a Kind Heart

Her innocence like a gentle breeze,
Touches souls, puts them at ease.
In every endeavor, she gives her all,
Praying silently, no one shall fall.

Prayers of a Gentle Soul

In every field, her efforts unfurled,
A prayer whispered for a kinder world.
May knowledge guide, manners refine,
Her gentle whispers, a beacon divine.

Ladders to The Sky

In soft murmurs innocence portrayed,
A child of eight, dreams cascading like a
cascade.
Mistakes unmade, yet taunts entwined,
A spirit pure, in shadows confined

The Garden of Dreams

Within her heart, a garden blooms,
Dreams in vibrant, fragrant plumes.
She tends to hope with tender care,
A sanctuary where wishes share.

A Symphony of Kindness

Her soul conducts a symphony,
Of kindness, a melody so free.
Despite the taunts that life may bring,
Compassion's song, she'll always sing.

Twist of Fate

Fifteen brings a twist in fate,
Dreams rerouted, yet hope innate.
Striding through a path unknown,
Destiny guides where seeds are sown.

A Dance in Shadows

On a chosen path, shadows dance,
Yet she twirls with bold expanse.
Graceful in struggles, a spirit untold,
In the shadow's midst, her strength unfolds.

Footprints in the Sand

Like footprints in the shifting sand,
Her kindness leaves a mark so grand.
Though storms may come and try to erase,
Love endures an unwavering grace.

Puzzle Pieces of Joy

Life's puzzle pieces she assembles,
Creating joy from scattered trembles.
A mosaic of laughter, piece by piece,
A masterpiece of bliss, never to cease.

Whispers of the Willow

A willow weeps in the quiet glade,
Her sorrows shared, not to fade.
In the weeping, strength she finds,
A resilience that eternally binds.

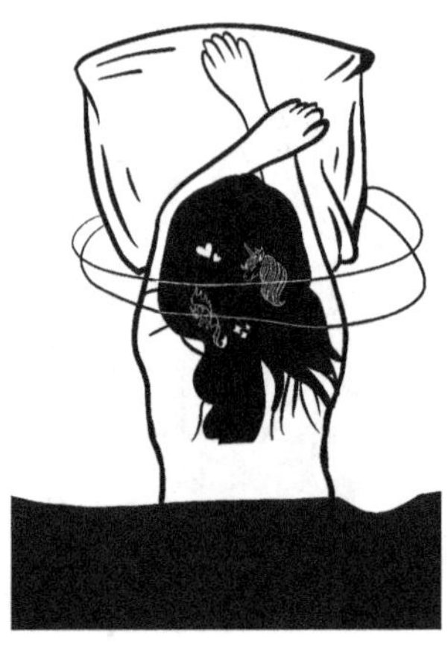

Balancing Acts

At eighteen, dreams soared so high,
Yet, life's twists made her question why.
Marriage, dreams, a tumultuous blend,
Yet, she balanced each till the very end.

Matrimony Veil

Vows exchanged a union tale,
Love and wounds within unveil.
Acceptance sought, love bestowed,
Life is a journey with secrets bestowed.

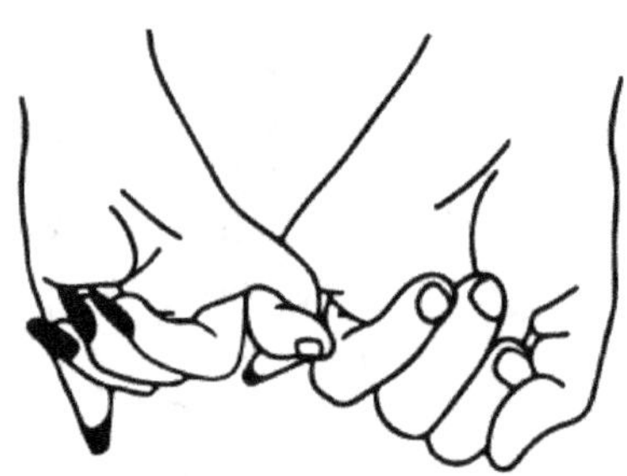

A Journey Of Dreams and Acceptance

Marriage, a journey, acceptance sought,
In every relation, battles fought.
She strived, she tried, to be embraced,
Yet, acceptance eluded, leaving her chaste.

The Unchosen Life

A different life, not of her choosing,
Yet, she donned it with grace, never losing.
Building castles of success and fame,
She played her part in life's endless game.

The Solo Journey

Alone she traveled, yet never alone,
With dreams to chase, a path to own.
In every duty, she gave her all,
A journey of triumphs, never a fall.

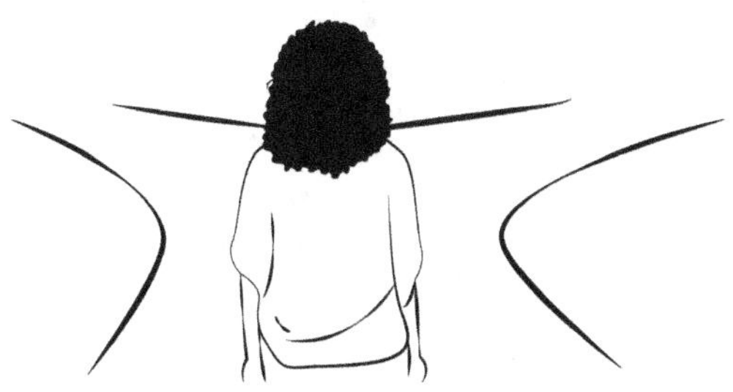

Echoes of Laughter

Echoes of laughter, like soft rain,
A balm for hearts, healing pain.
In every smile, she'd strive to create,
A symphony of joy, never too late.

Silent Serenade

In the quiet of night, under star's gentle gaze,
She waited, heart aflutter, in silent grace.
For a soul to sit beside her, in silence profound,
Where words were unnecessary, love whispers
abound.

Yearning Hearts

Yearning for a touch that speaks volumes untold,
In tender silence, their bond would unfold.
To feel wanted, appreciated, and adored,
In the stillness of companionship, her heart
soared.

Timeless Lessons

Lessons learned through joy and sorrow,
Echoing through a timeless tomorrow.
In every trial, a hidden grace,
A journey etched in life's vast space.

The Realization

One day, she woke, a truth unveiled,
This wasn't the life she had hailed.
Choices made, but not her own,
She carved new paths, seeds were sown.

A New Chapter Penned

With determination ablaze, she penned,
A new chapter where her dreams ascend.
Turning reality from every plight,
She shaped her world, bathed in light.

Eclipse of Trials

Trials eclipsed by the light of her will,
Resilience kindled an indomitable skill.
She rises above the darkest of nights,
A testament to her unwavering heights.

A Symphony of Relations

Relations and jobs, a symphony played,
With love and affection, the notes arrayed.
She embraced each note, in harmony,
Balancing life's complex melody.

A Symphony of Triumph

Triumph echoes in her soul's corridors,
Every challenge faced a tale that endures.
A symphony of strength, courage, and grace,
The crescendo of a triumphant embrace.

Sunrise Serenity

27

With every sunrise, a serenity unfolds,
A promise of warmth, as new tales are told.
She embraces the dawn with open arms,
A canvas of hope, where beauty charms.

Cocoon of Courage

Wrapped in a cocoon of courage tight,
She faces shadows with unyielding might.
In vulnerability, a strength she would find,
A metamorphosis of heart and mind.

Reflections in a Teardrop

In teardrops shed, reflections gleam,
A river of emotions, an endless stream.
Each droplet a story, pure and clear,
Unveiling truths she holds dear.

The Awakening Dawn

As dawn awakens, a new day begins,
Her story told, in whispers and grins.
Through every trial, she chose to stand,
A testament to life's gentle hand.

The Canvas of Tomorrow

Her life is a canvas, colors bold,
Dreams painted in stories untold.
With every stroke, a world anew,
A masterpiece in shades of dew.

Finding the Key within

With head held high, and smile aglow,
She walks with purpose, in radiance to show.
No longer seeking approval decree,
For within herself, she found the key.

Testament of Resilence

Each step she takes, a testament bold,
To resilience forged in the fire hold.
No more the victim, no more the pawn,
She has claimed her throne, at the break of
dawn.

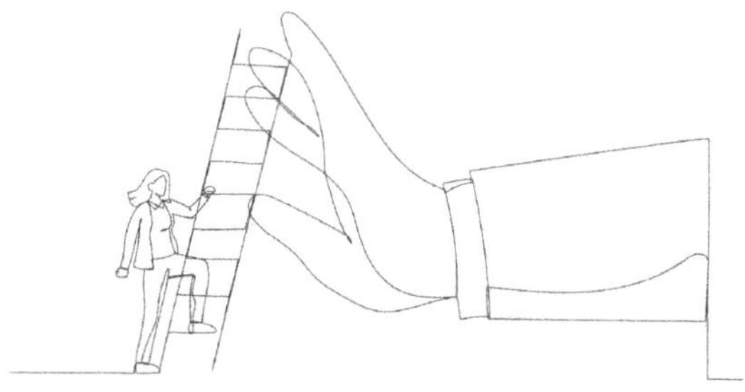

Claiming the Throne

Though doors may close, and silence may reign,
She wears her crown, free from disdain.
For in her heart, she knows her worth,
A queen reborn, from ashes of dearth.

Rise of the Queen

So let the world watch, as she ascends,
A beacon of strength, where hope transcends.
For in her journey, a truth is seen,
The rise of a queen, in the face of unseen.

The Path Chosen

Proud she stands, in the light of day,
Choosing the path of success, come what may.
No longer bound by sorrow's chains,
She has forged her destiny, where victory reigns.

Phoenix's Flight

She takes flight, a phoenix reborn,
From ashes of despair, her spirit sworn.
A final chapter, a tale's completion,
A phoenix's flight, a soul's sweet rendition.

Phrasing Life

"Life is a song," she softly said,
Phrasing each note, 'til the symphony's spread.
In every chapter, find your rhyme,
Create your music, in your own time.

The Greed for Dreams

In the depths of night, let dreams ignite,
A hunger fierce, a greedy sight.
For in the realm of aspirations high,
Greed for dreams shall touch the sky.

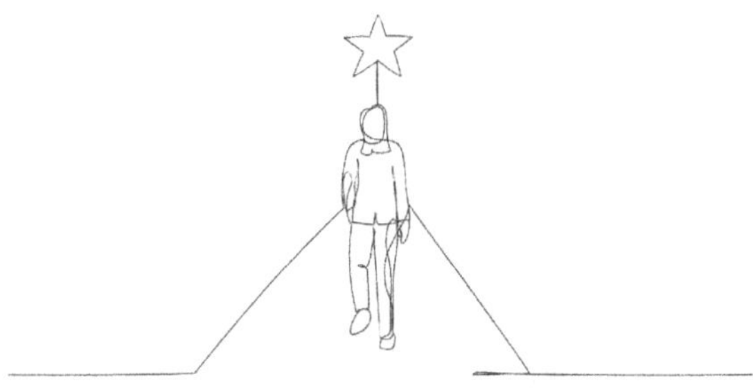

Embrace Self-Love

Before the world, thyself embrace,
In tender arms, find your place.
For love begins within the soul,
A journey towards the self, a sacred goal.

Identity's Forge

In the forge of time, identity's mold,
A tapestry of stories, yet untold.
Forge your name with fiery might,
In the annals of destiny, burn bright.

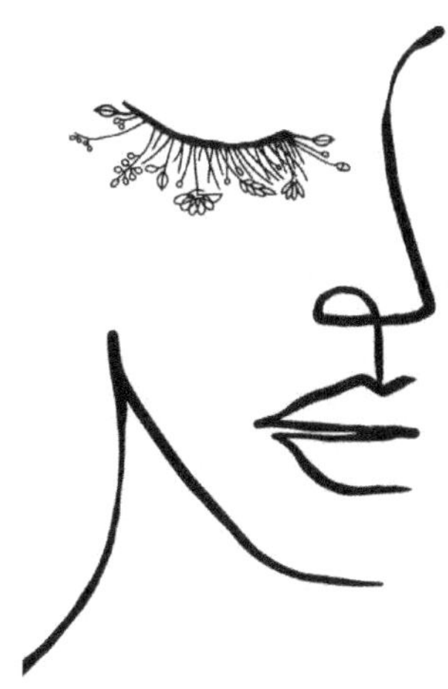

Speak Out

When silence reigns, and voices quake,
Let courage rise, a stand to take.
For in the echoes of truth unspoken,
Lies the power to mend what's broken.

Uphold Morals

Let not the shadows of doubt descend,
In the light of morals, let hearts mend.
For in the tapestry of right and wrong,
Stand firm, let integrity's song prolong.

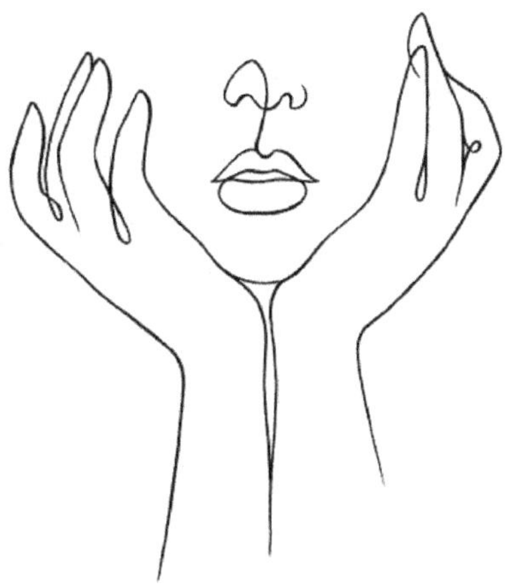

Authenticity's Anthem

In the tapestry of life, authenticity gleams,
Each soul a star in the vast cosmic streams.
Embrace your truth, let your uniqueness speak,
For when you are real, your essence peaks.

Whispers of a Gentle Soul

In whispers soft, a gentle soul confides,
Longing to speak what within her abides.
Yet shackled by fear, her words remain unsaid,
Her true desires locked within, tightly wed.

But learn from her plight, oh dear reader mine,
Let not your soul's voice be silenced by time.
Speak with courage, in tones calm and clear,
For life grants but one chance, hold it dear.

Embrace the moment, let truth take flight,
In the gentle whispers of your soul's light.
For regrets weigh heavy on hearts undone,
Seize the chance now, before the setting sun.

www.ingramcontent.com/pod-product-compliance
Lightning Source LLC
LaVergne TN
LVHW041234200726
843507LV00013B/2694